PUFFIN POETRY

TALKING TURKEYS

Benjamin Zephaniah was born and raised in Birmingham. He cannot remember a time when he wasn't creating poetry – *Talking Turkeys*, his first collection for children, was published in 1994, followed by *Funky Chickens* in 1996. In 1999 he wrote *Face*, the first of four gritty, realistic novels for teenagers. Benjamin is passionate about poetry and politics, and works tirelessly with many human and animal rights groups as well as political organizations throughout the world.

BENJAMIN ZEPHANIAH

LOVE HOP

TALKING TURKEYS

PUFFIN POETRY

PUFFIN BOOKS

UK | USA | Canada | Ireland | Australia
India | New Zealand | South Africa

Puffin Books is part of the Penguin Random House group of companies
whose addresses can be found at global.penguinrandomhouse.com.

puffinbooks.com

First published by Viking 1994
Published in Puffin Books 1995
Reissued in this edition 2015
001

Filmset in Sabon and Frutiger
Printed in Great Britain by Clays Ltd, St Ives plc

A CIP catalogue record for this book is available from the British Library

ISBN: 978–0–141–36296–0

www.greenpenguin.co.uk

Dedicated to the Earth _____

_____ and the children who care

CONTENTS

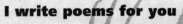

I write poems for you
And I hope that one day
You will write poems for me.
Read on and write soon.

TURKEY TALK

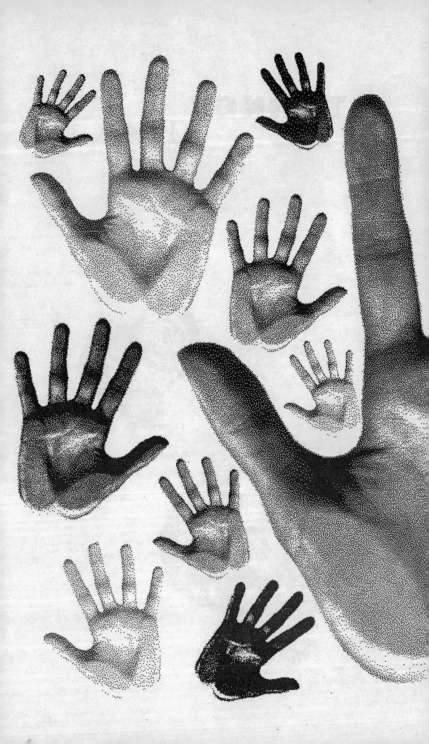

GREET TINGS

Assalaam Alaikum
Hola
Szia
Sat Srii Akaal
Wa Happen
Zdravo
Yia Sou
Merhaba
Hej
Yo
Sawast Dee Craap
Ciao
Zdravstvuyte
Endemenesh
Ahoj
Bonjour
Yassou
Shalom
Namaste
Dag
Guten Tag
Buenos Dias
Parev
Ehida
Selamat Datong
Dia Dhuit
Hallo
And Welcome

BODY TALK

Dere's a Sonnet
Under me bonnet
Dere's a Epic
In me ear,
Dere's a Novel
In me navel
Dere's a Classic
Here somewhere.
Dere's a Movie
In me left knee
A long story
In me right,
Dere's a shorty
Inbetweeny
It is tickly
In de night.
Dere's a picture
In me ticker
Unmixed riddims
In me heart,
In me texture
Dere's a comma
In me fat chin
Dere is Art.

Dere's an Opera
In me bladder
A Ballad's
In me wrist
Dere is laughter
In me shoulder
In me guzzard's
A nice twist.
In me dreadlocks
Dere is syntax
A dance kicks
In me bum
Thru me blood tracks
Dere run true facts
I got limericks
From me Mum,
Documentaries
In me entries
Plays on history
In me folk,
Dere's a Trilogy
When I tink of three
On me toey
Dere's a joke.

RUNNING

I reckon I could run de world,
I used to run me school,
Hundred metres an two hundred metres,
I could run up Mount Everest
Wid a drink,
I could run tings wid big words
Like,
INFRASTRUCTURE,
an
TELECOMMUNICATION,
A marathon? Easy.
I could run out of bounds,
I run wild all de time
I run tings nice...as dey sey in Jamaica,
Or cool...as dey sey in Iceland,
I could run de Universe...in verse
But I haven't been given a chance.
I will get my chance,
Politicians are running outta ideas,
Dat may mean dat we all, you and me,
I an I,
All of we, may hav to run our own lives,
Dats bad...as dey sey in New York,
Way out...as dey sey in space,
All right...as dey sey in

Llanfairpwllgwy

gyllgogerchwyrndrobwll-llantysiliogogogoch.

FEAR NOT

Wanna be in our gang?
We cause Peace,
Fighters fear us,
On de streets
We shout slogans
Like,
Peace an Luv
One race, de Human Race
Make Patties Not War
An
Kiss a lip.

We are very safe
Animal friendly
Flower power crazy
Whole wheat flour fans.
We are de listening gang,
We want yu to say yes,
More,
Do it,
Go save everything.

Our only enemy is Ignorance
When we see it we rap it
In questions,
Reasoning an openmindedness,
We recycle ideas
An produce true stories,
Your stories,
Her stories an his
stories,
Wid luv stories.

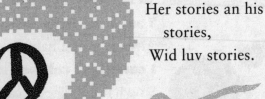

We hav no words for things like,
Join us,
We luv yu baby
We luv yu people
We luv yu grasshopper.

LITTLE SISTER

That's my little sister
Just five minutes old
Already seeking something
To bite and chew and hold,
That's my little sister
Already going bald
I can't just call her sister
So what will she be called?

I want to call her Carol
But all carols are hymns
I want to call her Jimmy
But I always visit gyms,
I want to call her spotty
But she may punch my nose
I will not call her Rosy
She don't look like a rose.

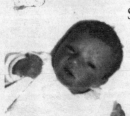

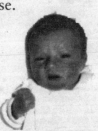

When I hear her crying
I want to call her *loud*
If she's the type for talking
I may call her a *crowd*,
If she's good at singing
I'll call her *nightingale*
If she keeps on grinning
She'll make the doctors wail.

The doctors called her beauty
But beauty is a horse
The nurses called her cutey
Being polite of course,
My Mummy and my Daddy
Just don't have an idea
We don't have a name ready
But we're so glad she's here.

FRIENDS

♥ **Funky monkey** in the tree
I like when you talk to me
What I really like the best
Is when you bang upon my chest.

♥ **Slippery snake** I am your mate
When all others hesitate
I'll be there right by your side
I am known to slip and slide.

22

♥ Hop along, croak croak, how ya doing **frog?**
No one understands our deep dialogue
People may laugh when they see us on the road
We must stick together
Monkey, snake, me, you and **toad**.

ACCORDING TO MY MOOD

I have *poetic* licence, i WriTe thE way i waNt.

i *drop* my **full stops** where *i* like...

MY CAPITAL Lete**R**s go where i li**KE**,

i **order** from **MY** PeN, i verse **the way** i like

(**i do** *my spelling write*)

Acording to My *MO*od.

i **HA**ve **p**oetic **licence**,

i put my **commers** where **i** like,,((O).

(((my brackets *are* **write**((

I REPEAT **WH**en i lik**E.**

i can't **go rong.**

i *look* and **i.c.**

It's rite.

i**I** REPEAT **WH**en i lik**E.** **i have**

poetic licence!

don't question me?**?**?*?*

ROYAL TEA

I went to Buckingham Palace today
To see where the Queen and her family stay
I went to Buckingham Palace today
To see the Queen's horses and men,
The Queen had gone shopping
A friend let us in
A very big chap with a very
    big grin
He put all the money I had in a tin
Security checked me and then,
He showed me a picture three hundred years old
Kept in a frame made of valuable gold
I told him I had one just like it indoors
And that I may sell it to help a good cause,
A chandelier he said was priceless was nice
I said my one's better and it has a price
I went in a big room and saw a big throne
Just like the one my Mum has at home.

I saw carpets on walls that were not for sale
I met the man who sorts out royal mail
I went in the room where the Queen has her balls
And in there I saw some more carpets on walls,
On high polished floors I had a good slide
I got a good telling off from the guide

That very big chap with the very big grin
Now looked even
    bigger was not smiling,
I said in his ear that I needed to
Pay a quick visit to the royal loo
It took fifteen minutes to get
    myself there
Upon the loo door it said
    'Kilroy waz ere'
Cameras filmed me on
    return to reception
I signed autographs for my royal connections
I left a note for the Queen saying she can
Visit me anytime she's in East Ham.

I went to Buckingham Palace today
To see where the Queen and her family stay
I went to Buckingham Palace today
To see royal things old and new,
It cost me eight fifty but no need to worry
If you visit me you don't need any money

There's no OBEs
but there's fresh tea
with honey
And I can take
photos of **you**.

HOW'S DAT

No Sir
X I don't play Cricket,
One time I try
Fearing a duck
I watch de ball fly towards me,
I recall every spin
An unforgettable air speed,
It bounced before me
Jus missing a two-day-old ant,
Up it cum
A red flash
Lick me finger so hard
I thought me finger would die.

Teacher tell me
X I am good at cricket,
I tell teacher
I am not,
Teacher tell me
We love cricket,
I tell teacher
Not me,
I want Trigonometry
Fe help me people,
Teacher tell me
I am a born Cricketer,
But I never...well only once,
X I don't play cricket.

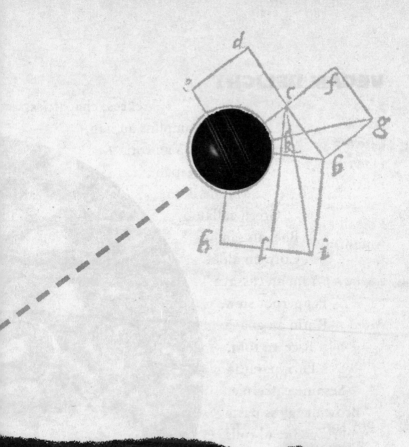

VEGAN DELIGHT

Ackees, chapatties
Dumplins an nan,
Channa an rotis
Onion uttapam,
Masala dosa
Green callaloo
Bhel an samosa
Corn an aloo.
Yam an cassava
Pepperpot stew,
Rotlo an guava
Rice an tofu,
Puri, paratha
Sesame casserole,
Brown eggless pasta
An brown bread rolls.

Soya milked muesli
Soya bean curd,
Soya sweet sweeties
Soya's de word,
Soya bean margarine
Soya bean sauce,
What can mek medicine?
Soya of course.

Soya meks yoghurt
Soya ice-cream,
Or soya sorbet
Soya reigns supreme,
Soya sticks liquoriced
Soya salads
Try any soya dish
Soya is bad.

Plantain an tabouli
Cornmeal pudding
Onion bhajee
Wid plenty cumin,
Breadfruit an coconuts
Molasses tea
Dairy free omelettes
Very chilli.
Ginger bread, nut roast
Sorrell, paw paw,
Cocoa an rye toast
I tek dem on tour,
Drinking cool maubi
Meks me feel sweet,
What was dat question now?
What do we eat?

OPEN MARKET

THE KIDS ON OUR BLOCK ARE OK
THEY'RE JUST LIKE THE KIDS FROM BOMBAY,
WHEN IT'S TIME TO SHOP
THEY'LL ORDER A LOT,
AND ASK THE SHOPKEEPER TO PAY.

THANKYOU - PLEASE CALL AGAIN SOON
04/02/94 18:04 001 1015 1934

MULTI-CULTURE

I really luv chapatties
I eat dem all de time,
Today Iqbal made ten of dem
An nine of dem were mine,
I am krazy over mangoes
I once grew a mango tree,
My mango tree grew chapatties
Especially for me.

FOOD FOR THOUGHT

Fed up with your old dog food
Try new '**Johnny**'.
Johnny contains all the
    goodness your dog needs.
Ideal for weight watching dogs,
Bite size pieces means less chewing for doggy
Lots of juicy gravy means doggy gets a stiff drink
And a happy dog means you're happy.
Look,
When confronted with 'some other dog food'
Your dog may wag its tail,
With new **Johnny** tails go krazy
Ears flip flop
Everything goes shaky, shaky, shaky,
Guard dogs don't fear
Johnny is here,
At prices some people can afford.

We spoke to Mrs Pal, a top breeder,
She said
'Get lost',
Then we spoke to Mr P.Chum,
He said
'I like it, I like it'.
Try new **Johnny** from Bite and
    Barkers,
Dogs would chose **Johnny**,
Johnny tastes so good.

*Bite and Barkers products
are not tested on animals.*

MR CANDYMAN

★ **Candyman, Candyman**
Give me a sweet
Sugar free
And carob coated
I deserve a treat
I've been working so hard
Counting all me toes
Looking at me garden
Watching how it grows.
Dear Mr Candyman
I don't have ten pence
But I may just sell dis poem
If it can make sense,
If I even sell one line
You can eat with me
Or we can buy a seed
And plant an apple tree.

★ **Thanks Mr Candyman**
It's a lovely colour
I think I may cut it in half
And share it with me brother,
If me brother likes it
He may just buy me poem
We're poor but we do part exchange
That's how we keep going.

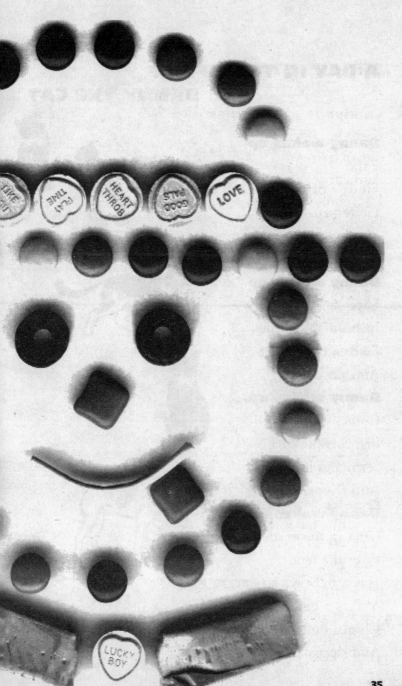

A DAY IN THE LIFE OF DANNY THE CAT

Danny wakes up
Eats
Finds a private place in the garden,
He returns
Plays with the plants
And sleeps.
Danny wakes up
Eats
Inspects the garden
Finds a cosy place
And sleeps.
Danny wakes up
Comes indoors
Inspects the carpet
Scratches himself
And sleeps.
Danny wakes up
Goes in the garden
Over the fence
Has a fight with Ginger
Makes a date with Sandy
Climbs on to next door's shed
And sleeps.

Danny wakes up
Comes indoors
Rubs up the chair leg
Rubs up a human leg
Sharpens his claws
On a human leg
Eats
And sleeps.
Danny wakes up
Eats

Watches a nature programme
Finds a private place in the garden,
Finds Sandy in next door's garden
Next door's dog finds Danny
Sandy runs north
Danny runs home
Eats an sleeps.

Danny wakes up
Checks for mice
Checks for birds
Checks for dogs
Checks for food
Finds a private place in the garden
Eats
And sleeps.

Danny has hobbies,
Being stroked
Car watching
And smelling feet

He loves life,
Keeps fit
And keeps clean,
Every night he covers himself
In spit,
Then he eats
And sleeps.

Benji

Danny

DRIVOSAURUS REX

The dinosaurs are back
Working at Hollywood
Now they are not flesh and bone
They're plastic, foam and wood
The dinosaurs are here
I saw one on a bus
As I was on the way to play
At Dinosaurs 'R' Us.

They came from Noah's Ark
Unto Jurassic Park
When they ete you can bet
They did some great big
Barks,
Then from Jurassic Park
Some came into our homes
In big boxes of cereals
With added rocks and stones.

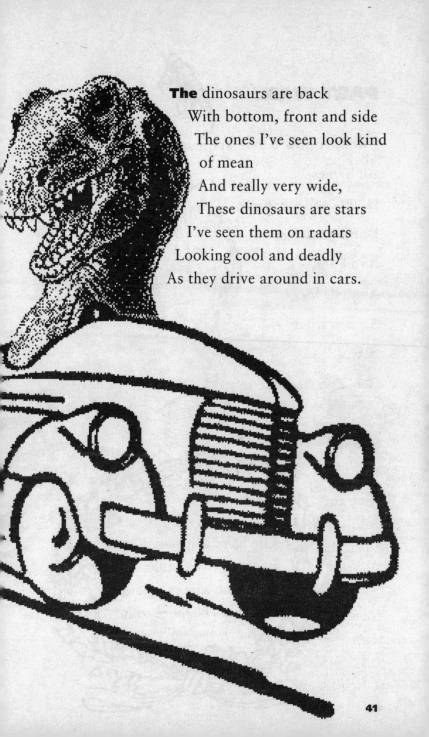

The dinosaurs are back
  With bottom, front and side
  The ones I've seen look kind
  of mean
  And really very wide,
  These dinosaurs are stars
  I've seen them on radars
Looking cool and deadly
As they drive around in cars.

PART WAN

I wonder how babies are made,

All babies

Homosapien babies,

Donkey babies,

Bird babies.

Animals kiss

An den what

Babies.

Dere mus be more to it.

PART TWO

Life has its ups an downs
Even captives smile
I wonder why people die?
Dere mus be more to it.

WORDOLOGY

Sociologists

Physicists

Archaeologists

And

Anthropologists

Like

Dieticians

Rhetoricians

Mathematicians

And

Politicians

Are simple people,

Help them.

DE GENERATION RAP

▶ Dat guy **BAD**
He's *kicking*,
He's *wicked*,
CRUCIAL,
Cums round *here*
Wida **smiley** pon his face,
He CHILLS out,
Slides round,
Mekin circles,
He's **safe**.

▶ **Dis** sista hard
She's *irie*,
MENTAL
RESPECT due,
She steps *cool*
Trods *easy*,
Hangs **tuff**,
Big up
An *vitalistic*.

When him pass thru

HARD VIBES,

Him *wild*,

Is a **neat** dude

SLICK geeza

A *natural* bro.

Made up.

She jus **OOW**,

Streetwise G,

She's **covered**

Fit, *Irie*,

X.

People on de **streets**

Luv dem so much,

Dem **jus call** dem

Drr Read full.

SOLIDARITY

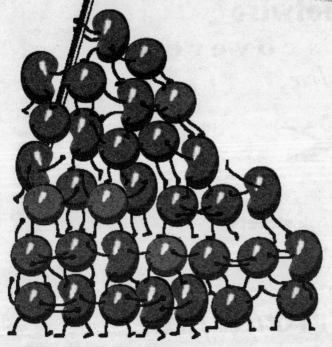

An army of militant greens

In bio-degradable genes

Shout 'Give peas a chance

An lettuce all dance

In unity wid butter beans'.

MEDIEVAL RELIGIOUS TRIBAL CHANT

Here we go

Here we go

Here we go

(Please repeat)

WHO'S WHO

I used to think **nurses**
Were women,
I used to think **police**
Were men,
I used to think **poets**
Were boring,
Until **I** became one of **them.**

Poet

49

RAP CONNECTED

We were born to rap
We were born to dance
We were born to sing
We are Queens an Kings
We were born to live de life dat we luv
We were born to luv de life dat we live,
We were born to twist

We were born to shout
We can keep it in
We can hang it out
We got riddim in us mate

Get infected,
Shout it loud,
We are connected.

We were born to share
An hav fun whilst here,
So if you don't care
Go somewhere you square,
If you are aware
You will be respected
We all share the air and
We are connected.

We are black an brown
We are white an sound
We have pride of place
We are on de case
We are wild an tame
We are all de same

Sister, brother, kid,
We are connected.

A KILLER LIES

> He's a Fox Hunter, he said
'Foxes need controlling, they spread germs
They're always mating.'
I think he's exaggerating,
He's a Fox Hunter, he said
'They're wild animals, they eat lambs and they eat
chickens.'
He needs chickens for his kitchen.

> He calls foxes beast,
But he collects their teeth,
He kills thousands every year
Once he whispered in me ear,
'It will kill you with its bite
That is why fox hunting's right,
Can't you sense they are evil
So unlike hunting people,
They are the enemy of our community
I love it when they're caught
And they make such good sport,
I never tasted one
When our hounds get them they're gone,
I am good at this you know
I'm a kind of Hunt hero.'

He's a Fox Hunter
His Daddy taught him well
When his hounds scent de smell
Excitement meks him yell,
He's a Fox Hunter
Know him by his killer eyes
Something dead must be his prize
He's de kind dat's **civilized.**

HEROES

Heroes are funny people, dey are lost an found
Sum heroes are brainy an sum are muscle-bound,
> Plenty heroes die poor an are heroes
> after dying
> Sum heroes mek yu smile when yu
> feel like crying.
Sum heroes are made heroes as a political trick
Sum heroes are sensible an sum are very thick!
Sum heroes are not heroes cause dey do not play de
  game
A hero can be young or old and have a silly name.
Drunks an sober types alike hav heroes of dere kind
Most heroes are heroes out of sight an out of mind,
Sum heroes shine a light upon a place where
  darkness fell
Yu could be a hero soon, yes, yu can never tell.
So if yu see a hero, better treat dem wid respect
Poets an painters say heroes are a prime subject,
Most people hav heroes even though some don't
  admit
I say we're all heroes if we do our little bit.

BEYOND DE BELL

Yu push
Yu shove
Believing
School moves round **yu**,
Yu spy an lie
Believing
Tings control by **yu**,
What mek **yu** tink like dat?
Never mind
Academic ability
Concentration span
I.Q. business
Yu big in de playground,
Never mind
People who
Don't push an shove,
Yu do.

Table may turn
Yu may be pushed,
An macho boy
Yu may lose **yu** watch
Yu ill gained sweet money
Yu bigheadedness,
Table may turn
Yu may be shoved
Den walked over
By an army
Of carers

Teaching lessons,
We don't want dat now
Do we.

Yu are not respected
Yu are other tings,
People do talk behind yu back
Whatever **yu** say,
We all have problems
But
Dere are people who will talk to **yu**
If **yu** won't talk to yuself.

Yu grab an slap
An won't give back
Believing
It's over at four,
By day **yu** taunt
At night **yu** haunt,
Believing
Yu rule OK,
What mek yu tink like dat?
Is it
Parents,
Dreams,
Bigger bullies
Or television,
Who do we blame,
An
What mek yu tink like dat?

CIVIL LIES

Dear Teacher,

When I was born in Ethiopia
Life began,
As I sailed down the Nile civilization began,
When I stopped to think universities were built,
When I set sail
Asians and true Americans sailed with me.

When we traded nations were built,
We did not have animals,
Animals lived with us,
We had so much time
Thirteen months made our year,
We created social services
And cities that still stand.

So teacher do not say
Colombus discovered me
Check the great things I was doing
Before I suffered slavery.

Yours truly,

Mr Africa

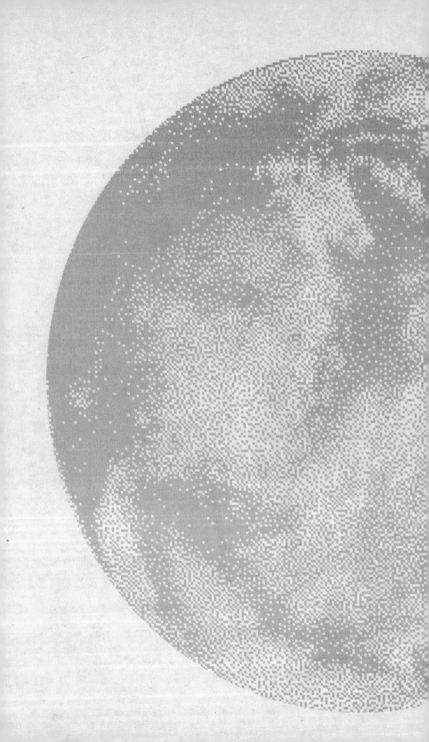

Poet

POEMS

FROM

THE

LAST

PERSON

ON

EARTH

FOR SALE

Looking for a bargain
Come on down
It's the Sale of the Century
Look around
There are sights to see
And places to be
With way out cosmic activity
This is a deal that you can't refuse
The kind of bet you cannot lose
So come on down
The price is right
I got to sell this thing tonight.

Chorus

Roll up, Roll up, Planet for Sale
Roll up, Planet for Sale.

Free of living things that roam
Free of people and ozone
I invite you to test my ware
Free of any atmosphere
Enjoy yourself as you get poorly
With no sign of a creepy crawly
I promise you will find no trees

And no flowers to make you sneeze.
Little Bo Peep has gone with her sheep
And little Jack Horner dissolved in a corner,
That Donald Duck has run out of luck
And Paddington Bear is no longer here
The Owl and the Pussy Cat went to sea
Then got lost in infinity.
Alive Alive no, Alive Alive no
Cockles and Mussels are not,
And no snow.

Chorus

**Roll up, Roll up, Planet for Sale
Roll up, Planet for Sale.**

Looking for a bargain, check this planet
Not a thing is moving on it
Just for you I'll do a deal
I'll swap it for a decent meal.

A BEETLE CALLED DEREK

There once was a Beetle called Derek
Who lived in a forest on Earth
And this little Beetle called Derek
Was really attracted to dirt,
She did not carry no weapons
Except what she naturally got
She did not have no possessions
But she could look after her lot.

The forest protected our Derek
Predators came and they went,
This was no reason to panic
Cause this was with Nature's consent,
She was related to Wind and Fire
A sister of necessity,
She was related to Earth and Water
A distant cousin to me.
Doctors could not work out Derek
Derek had secrets she kept,
Then came the white coated bandits
Scientists seeking all they could get,
Her home was robbed to make paper
And that got the climate upset,
Cows would graze to make burgers
The cows never made a profit!!

Derek was taken for granted ✸
By selfish, non-beetle people,
Some supporters of Derek demanded
An end to what we called Evil,
Handouts could not solve the problem alone
So I called out the Eco-Police,
But we could not win the fight on our own
Now Derek my friend is deceased.

There once was a Beetle called Derek ✸
Who lived in a forest on Earth,
Nobody knew where she came from
A kind of mysterious birth,
I built a memorial to Derek
Hoping that it may be seen,
I hope when I die I'll see Derek,
In a heaven organic and green.

BEAT IT

I broke my world record

I am famous for it

But now I am so bored

Cos I have no music.

PETS CONTROL

We moved into a house
We kicked de animals out,
Den we got our pets
An signed on at de vets,
We den called wild life strays
Zoos captured dem,
We gazed,
Wild life made great TV,
How civilized were we?

MEMORIES

I recall a time
Not long ago
When sheep would roam
    around here,
If you were nice and friendly
You could get close to a deer,
Foxes, rabbits
Wild and free
We had so much potential,
But we did not live in harmony
And that was detrimental.
I take no blame
I did not do it
I was an innocent child,
My roots are very vegan
I like my animals wild,
I take no blame
I did not do it
I wrote to all the rulers,
I took a stand,
I loved the land
How I loved the Animal Kingdom.

I saw people training dogs
To make the doggies violent
Rulers of the land made dog
owners
Buy a licence,
I saw furs of animals
Upon human backs
I saw furs of animals
Being used as mats,
It happened here, I saw it
I called it Human Madness
I saw friends disappear
Imagine all my sadness,
I shouted from all high places
Let us not do this crime,
Nobody listened to me
Nobody had the time.

Memories don't leave like people do
I miss the kangaroo,
I recall great big trees,
I need these memories.

THINK ME

I want to be
In someone's mind
For ever
And ever
All right,
I want my picture taken
I must be someone's thought,
Somebody somewhere
Dream of me
I want to be
Remembered.

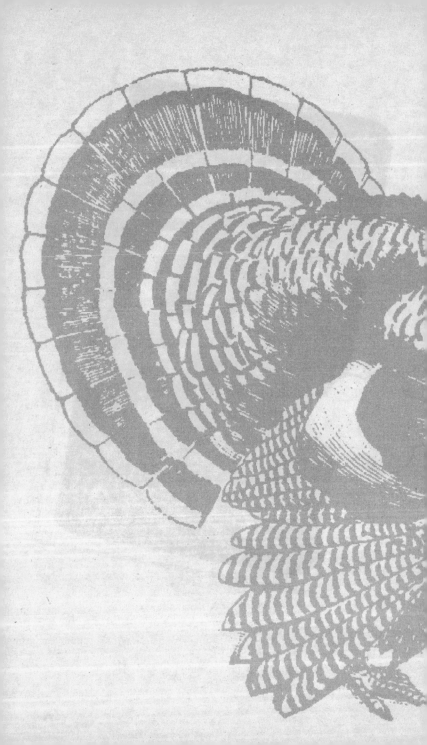

MORE TURKEY TALK

I

If
Big
Boys
Don't
Cry
'
'

Why
Do
I
?
.

LETTERS

I keep reading luv letters
So I won't feel alone,
I'll publish it an frame it
If I get one of me own.

KISS AN TELL

I kissed a girl
She nicked me tongue
It swept me off me feet,
It blew de air from out me lungs
An me heart missed a beat
Me liver quivered
Me legs shivered
Me head started swelling
Me eyes rolled back
Me back went crack
Den she started yelling,

'Clean your teeth!'

OVER DE MOON

Dere's a man on de moon
He's skipping an stuff,
Dere's a man on de moon
He looks very tuff,
Dere's a man on de moon
An he's all alone,
Dere's a man on de moon
His wife is at home.

He's dancing around
To real moony music,
He carries his air
He knows how to use it,
He waves to his wife
Still on Planet E,
She's waving back
But he cannot see.

De man on de moon is so clever,
He has sum ideas to persue,
His chewing gum can last fe ever
His fast food is already chewed.

Dere's a man on de moon
He has a spaceship,
Dere's a man on de moon
An we payed fe it,
Dere's a man on de moon
His mission ain't done,
Dere's a man on de moon
He's after de Sun.

MOVIE MADNESS

Jellybean one waz a blockbuster
Jellybean two waz a flop
Jellybean three a disaster
Jellybean four cost a lot
Jellybean five waz a miss take
Jellybean six was withdrawn
Jellybean seven a headache
Jellybean eight made us yawn.
Jellybean nine was just too much
Jellybean ten came and went
Jellybean films made me bankrupt
Because my film money's all spent.

FAIR PLAY

Mirror mirror on the wall
Could you please return our ball
Our football went through your crack
You have two now
Give one back.

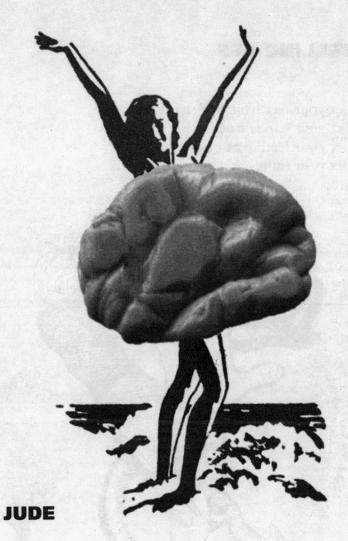

JUDE

Dere waz a cool dude called Jude
Who waz terribly awfully rude,
She spread bubble gum
All over her bum
An now she is stuck in de nude.

TELLING OFF

☞ Get your feet from **off** that table
Get your hands **out** of that pie
Get your teeth **out** of that apple
Get your things and say **goodbye**.

LUV SONG

I am in luv wid a hedgehog
I've never felt dis way before
I have luv fe dis hedgehog
An everyday I luv her more an more,
She lives by de shed
Where weeds an roses bed
An I just want de world to know
She makes me glow.

I am in luv wid a hedgehog
She's making me hair stand on edge,
So in luv wid dis hedgehog
An her friends
Who all live in de hedge
She visits me late
An eats off Danny's plate
But Danny's a cool tabby cat
He leaves it at dat.

I am in luv wid a hedgehog,
She's gone away so I must wait
But I do miss my hedgehog
Everytime she goes to hibernate.

EYE SEE

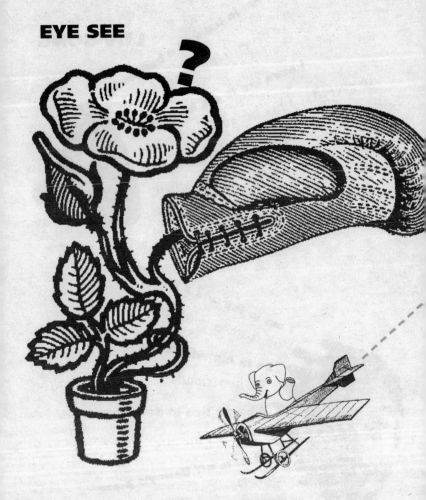

I've never seen flowers fight

It seems

Not all living things do,

I've never seen poodles get dressed

I have seen

Many well dressed,

84

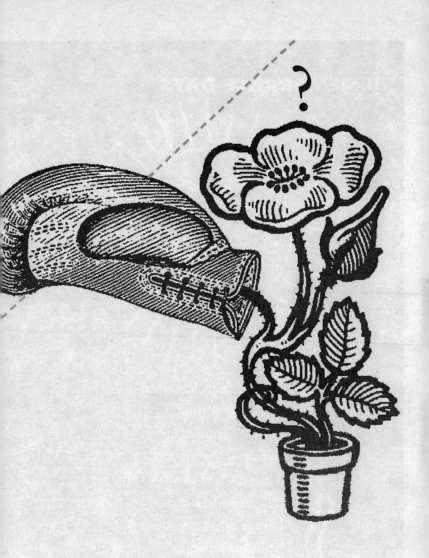

I have seen elephants fly

It seems

Not all people see what I see,

I've never seen a blind person lost

It seems

Only the sighted lose their way.

REMEMBRANCE DAYS

Ramadan in Pakistan
Is a special time
On Christmas Day in
Jamaica
The sun will always shine,
Diwali in India
Brings all the colours out
And don't forget
In Tibet
Each day
A Poet
Shouts.

EVERYDAY

Happy Birthday.

Today

You

Are

One

Day

Older,

Let's celebrate.

TALKING TURKEYS!!

Be nice to yu turkeys dis christmas
  Cos turkeys jus wanna hav fun
  Turkeys are cool, turkeys are wicked
  An every turkey has a Mum.
  Be nice to yu turkeys dis christmas,
  Don't eat it, keep it alive,
  It could be yu mate an not on yu plate
Say, Yo! Turkey I'm on your side.

I got lots of friends who are turkeys
An all of dem fear christmas time,
Dey wanna enjoy it, dey say humans destroyed it
An humans are out of dere mind,
Yeah, I got lots of friends who are turkeys
Dey all hav a right to a life,
Not to be caged up an genetically made up
By any farmer an his wife.

Turkeys jus wanna play reggae
Turkeys jus wanna hip-hop
Can yu imagine a nice young turkey saying,
'I cannot wait for de chop'?
Turkeys like getting presents, dey wanna
  watch christmas TV,
Turkeys hav brains an turkeys feel pain
In many ways like yu an me.

I once knew a turkey called
Turkey
He said 'Benji explain to me please,
Who put de turkey in christmas
An what happens to christmas trees?'
I said, 'I am not too sure turkey
But it's nothing to do wid Christ Mass
Humans get greedy an waste more dan need be
An business men mek loadsa cash.'

Be nice to yu turkey dis christmas
Invite dem indoors fe sum greens
Let dem eat cake an let dem partake
In a plate of organic grown beans,
Be nice to yu turkey dis christmas
An spare dem de cut of de knife,
Join Turkeys United an dey'll be delighted
An yu will mek new friends '**FOR LIFE**'.

CHRISTMAS WISE

☆ All I **want** fe christmas is world peace
I **don't want** loads a food dat I really can't eat
All I **want** fe christmas is a long holiday
An a house in Jamaica where I can stay.
I **don't want** kisses under mistletoe from
Sloppy people I don't know,
I **won't** be putting out nu stocking cos
I **don't** wear de tings,
I **won't** be cutting down nu christmas trees,
I like dem living.

☆ All I **want** fe christmas is dis planet for ever
Fully complete wid its ozone layer
All I **want** fe christmas is friends and...
No more records from Status Quo,
I **don't want** a white christmas an I bet
We'll get nu more of dem cos of de Greenhouse effect,
An I **reckon** at christmas we create too much waste
Maybe a green christmas is more to my taste.
All I **want** fe christmas is sum honesty
About de wisdom of christmas
An how it should be
All I **want** fe christmas is clean air,
But I reckon I won't get none
An I don't think dat's fair.

SUNNYSIDE UP

When people
See people
Reading up
Side Down,
They think,
Maybe,
The reader
Can't read,
But
You should
Smile now,
Because you
Have found
A poem
That's out
To mislead.

ONCE UPON A TIME

I dreamt of living in a great big house
With a great big cat and a great big mouse
With a great big cupboard
Full of great big pears
I would grow great big
Without any cares.
Me great big hair on me great big head
Would feel great tucked into
Me great big bed
In me great bedroom
I would have great fights
With me big shadow
Who is really bright,
A great big sun shine would wake me up
I would drink great juice from a great big cup
And a great breakfast would make me feel great
And me school teachers would be always late.

I would speak great poems
With me great big voice
Great big hugs and kisses
Would make me feel nice
This great world would work together
    as a team
I would live for ever
In me great big dream.

93

INDEX OF FIRST LINES

It all started with a Scarecrow

Puffin is over seventy years old.
Sounds ancient, doesn't it? But Puffin has never been
so lively. We're always on the lookout for the next big
idea, which is how it began all those years ago.

Penguin Books was a big idea from the mind of
a man called Allen Lane, who in 1935 invented
the quality paperback and changed the world.
**And from great Penguins, great Puffins grew,
changing the face of children's books forever.**

The first four Puffin Picture Books were hatched in 1940 and the
first Puffin story book featured a man with broomstick arms called
Worzel Gummidge. In 1967 Kaye Webb, Puffin Editor, started the
Puffin Club, promising to **'make children into readers'**.
She kept that promise and over 200,000 children became devoted
Puffineers through their quarterly instalments of *Puffin Post*.

Many years from now, we hope you'll look back and
remember Puffin with a smile. **No matter what your age
or what you're into, there's a Puffin for everyone.**
The possibilities are endless, but one thing is for sure:
whether it's a picture book or a paperback, a sticker book
or a hardback, **if it's got that little Puffin
on it – it's bound to be good.**